NEW VRINDABAN

NEW VRINDABAN
POEMS

JACOB STRAUTMANN

FOUR WAY BOOKS
TRIBECA

LIBRARY OF CONGRESS CATALOGING-IN-PUBLICATION DATA

Library of Congress Cataloging-in-Publication Data

Names: Strautmann, Jacob, author.
Title: New Vrindaban / Jacob Strautmann.
Description: [New York] : Four Way Books, 2024.
Identifiers: LCCN 2024000661 (print) | LCCN 2024000662 (ebook) | ISBN
   9781961897069 (trade paperback) | ISBN 9781961897076 (epub)
Subjects: LCGFT: Poetry.
Classification: LCC PS3619.T74345 N49 2024 (print) | LCC PS3619.T74345
   (ebook) | DDC 811/.6--dc23/eng/20240111
LC record available at https://lccn.loc.gov/2024000661
LC ebook record available at https://lccn.loc.gov/2024000662

This book is manufactured in the United States of America and printed on acid-free paper.

Four Way Books is a not-for-profit literary press. We are grateful for the assistance
we receive from individual donors, public arts agencies, and private foundations
including the NEA, NEA Cares, Literary Arts Emergency Fund, and the
New York State Council on the Arts, a state agency.

We are a proud member of the Community of Literary Magazines and Presses.

for my bandmates

SIDE ONE

SIDE TWO

01.
Transiting Planet

Our daughter always slept fist
    To ear, beckoning
An exhaustive catalog pass:
Red clay, black bear, green

Valise, ancestors like songs
    In orbit, like filled-in
Jagged inked-on scripture.
Fatherhood strengthened my spine,

Slowly the brave alloys fused,
    Beard white as a bleached bib,
Pressures of 24,000 atmospheres.
We left our keys on the mantle,

Were gifted a son in the spring—
    Who wouldn't breathe, who
Was lifted watery over a metal table,
His face covered with their rescue,

And when he wailed, his mother bled
    The released fists of the room;
The doctor smiled behind her mask
And stitching. He would sail away

Across an unknown channel,
    The future a dog star signaling.
Whoever finds us should know
We arrive like this—pulse by pulse.

02.
Under the Velvet Elvis

It's carried over the 50,000 watt
Beacon of Six O'Clock Mine Reports whose dark
Doxologies call to who will and who won't work—
Before the power goes down a second time.

Prayers and candles gig across a wall
Slick with mirrors. The floor's meticulously
Swept plywood whispers like a devotee,
As a nylon smock twisted becomes a swan

Resting on a swivel back, third chair down.
But in repose, deeper, the owner's son
Reclined, head back at the hair washing station,
Hasn't moved at all. He's been there for weeks.

Having draped him in flowers, lit the incense,
Mother and aunt, who brought him to this office,
Claim a honey sweet scent, or a black licorice,
Or the vapor of twice baked bread will rise

Over his cheekbones taut as an oil drum.
His curls drift, rigid, in the flickering bath,
The petals beside him floating. There is a faith
Arrived at when any steel mill shuts its doors

Or mine is sealed with only a sign and chain
To hold the wageless back from their guerdons:
Sacrifice binds us to the chorus. Unions
Bargain as the young lie back in their living graves.

And so the sisters keep an empty business,
Watch over the register that will be opened,
Wash his hair with ginseng, their charge attend,
His waxen lip worked nightly, rockabilly.

Below the brushed images of The King
Sounds of a hundred country stations revel
For all the young ones (all their dreams fulfill),
Hushed as sleeping Adams. The static jumps.

One can almost make out guitar, a man
Of conviction; the other, who he would
Have married had the economy allowed.
Hear them singing what he could have been.

03.
Passado

When the sun gobos his weight
To a pressing point, a sword slips
Under the arm of a new groom,
And scratches Mercutio dead.
Barely a teenager when I first

Sat back from a page running
Too slowly for the surgeon,
I felt the parry of a man fighting
For his friend, knew I was none,
No Mercutio, no one Mercutio

To me. When I found a man
Who would passado for his dozen
Friends as easily as smoke
A pack of reds or clip his locks
Before the dorm room windows

Fully confident in rumors of
His beauty, I asked who he was
Doing it for, assumed he tallied
Us in his starry counting house.
We could not love him to the depth

He gave us—his was as vertical
As a well, wide as a chapel door.
Whatever makes us careless,
He kept it hidden, pulled it closed
Like a curtain that let slip

Scenes of preening, drugging.
We stand stock still in the wings
This green season of suicides,
Suddenly middle-aged
And always his audience.

04.
Sean's Song

Your name bangs open, a bell in middle life,
But your name won't ring, or husband your return,
    Or father unharmed
The man we love: the kite of a name
    (Not the weight of a hand)
Worries to nothing in a tall magnolia.
Branches will blanch the city of Cleveland
    As you resist
The startled passel calling to
    Where you struck first.

05.

The First Flowers Bloom in
Southern West Virginia along Stream Banks

A poem found in the WV Encyclopedia
In the prose of William N. Grafton

1

Coltsfoot begins to cover roadsides with yellow:
Lookalike cousin, dandelion, the yards and fields.

Pink-striped flowers of spring beauties
And the white and blue hepatica.

Skunk cabbage produces heat to melt the ice
And pushes up its quaint green cap
With a purple pedestal inside.

Pink and white flowers of trailing arbutus
Peek out from under leaves flattened by winter snows.

2

White flowers of Clintonia,
Plumelily, anemones, mayapple,
Twinleaf, bloodroot, squirrel corn,
Dutchman's breeches, toothworts,
Stonecrop, foamflower, sweet cicely,
And saxifrage seem to dominate.

3

Mayapple is recognized by the large white flower,
Unique umbrella-like leaves. The low-growing stonecrop,
Three spikes of flowers and succulent leaves similar to cactus.

Dutchman's breeches, a pair of pants hanging upside down.
Its cousin, squirrel corn, has a white flower resembling
A boiled kernel and root bulbs that look like yellow corn.

Yellow flowers of buttercups, fawn lilies, bellworts,
And golden-knees. Marsh marigold, also yellow,
Grows in wet areas in the high mountains.

06.
Every Fleck of Russet

In a pasture orchard, the quarter horses
Strip the flaking bark, and the scent of asters
Spangle the hillside, buoying the crabapples,
Teasing soft muzzles through the living balloons,
> *Freely you have received; freely give.*

Stinger auxiliaries drive them back—shod hooves
Fling black dirt at a child's face, mother's hand
Pressing him to earth, but not instant as fate,
That day of seven years anointing him
> *Freely you have received; freely give.*

Flies on a rag, and she cradles her son—
"Crawl from that vessel that holds you like a mother."
She spits on her finger and washes the rings
Around his eyes, words mouthed that make
> *Freely you have received; freely give.*

Futures unravel and the whole world dies
To live in him again. All he knows is the sky,
Panicked horses, smoke pouring from a torn
Open tree, laughter over the buckets of fruit.
> *Freely you have received; freely give.*

07.
Blackberry Purposes

Sunday, as ever, I visited
His porch, steam escaping the pie tin,
And he ate while I spoke, grey whiskers
He missed in a half-hearted shave swerved

Around the shadows that carved his mouth.
I, well-aware of his dancing eye,
Told how Friday I fell in the street,
Dress torn at the hem, muck up my back,

Little time to wash my arms before
Proctoring the girls a silly test,
A capstone Finishing Schools require.
"What do you claim as yours?" I asked them.

"Life is not performing for others,
No matter who is watching"—to prove
My words, a finished woman is not
What they think, I showed them my backside,

And he laughed, blackseed molars open,
Eyes squeezed shut, wrapped in a coughing fit,
Gripping the chair's strength, my wrist, to say
His episode would pass. Could have left

Him well-enough, but then I told how
I would marry a man from Wheeling,
And he didn't smile or wish me well
And put down his fork on his plate.

08.
Mildred's Flight

Love was the airline ticket, a grown son in California,
And you walking the length of the cabin,

Its long columns of seats not the single row
You always arranged buried deep in the wings.

> 67 years mistaking the view:
> The fearlessness you called up
> To expect the sleeping earth would
> Take leave at your feet, the clouds

> Shearing away from the swing
> Of your chair back, broad sky.
> You told me how children
> Ran into the street to catch

Sight of a plane, a stitch of silver above the Ohio
So rare in those days, and the Depression on,

And maybe that's why you waited so long
To leave us below, sure the X you saw up there

Was too thin crown to foot to hold more
Than one man aloft. But I'll hold you there,

Millie, marveling at what you can see of the wings,
The widows of the first class stored bravely inside.

09.
Patternicities (Lunar View J2857)

At the terminator, wreckage flickers
Before the lines dissipate in a camouflage

Light. The long tooth of noon is on the surface;
Reprieve—name of her blinding horn.
But even in this overload

Closing an eye keeps
Nothing out, ballet of three bodies felt
More than seen anyway: mystery, cacoëthe,
And something that would burn with

An oxidizer deployed. Gravity's
Unsurmountable narrative continues, so wait
The period allotted. The next time around

Debris fields will stand out in their sunrise,
Digest holding everyone accountable.

10.
Belmont Amor

Town-sized drama of flip-flapping awnings
In the head toss of a downgraded tropical storm.
Birds lash by. Men in their fire aspect
Who will dance au naturale on Leonard,
Barter ewel for beer and butter cakes.

A jury of women assemble in the center,
Oboes, sousaphones held aloft,
With detailed forecasts, simulations run.
The last of us snagged the train, but I stayed on,
And for a moment I was the only one

They were talking to in Paradise.
When shall I find you in all this noise?
How will I return the veil blown free
And hopping the track?

At the Clay Pit Pond, a skein of geese
Synchronize a rowdy entrance:
All their toiling festoons the hedges,
Avenues pavement-dark with possibility.

11.
Mountain Latchkey, 1983

Hellbent for the Blue Ridge Parkway
She never told anyone she was going,
Never claimed to be in their number,
Where mystery was a pair of glasses
Thickening on a creek's wrecked bank.

Are we, half of us asks, *fooling ourselves?*
As the decades sink knotted as snakes
Fastened in a canvas sack. Needlework
Of sunlight would not slip through these
Polaroids guardian angels under- or

Overexposed. Newspaper clippings give
No new evidence, creased, unsealed,
Something that looks like her face
On the edge of the frame, always leaving.
But in this one: at an Airstream's drop down,

Moonscape (our best guess) stretched all
Directions, she watches us, willfully,
Out of the veil of the flashbulb,
Bomber jacket, her Dostoyevsky
Bangs, all of her cards on the table.

12.

Epimetheus in the Fall of the Year

I'm suffering my own mid-winter butchering.
My little kids sleep. My wife grocery getting.
Cat getting fucked behind the garage.

Destiny appeared backwards in me,
A resolution to return to the scene,
Someone for whom the howling of a train

Is most cleanly meant: desperately known
After it passes, all the moonlit roofs shaken,
Mortgaged suburban American hearts.

What if we died with the end of December,
Reborn on the first, forgetful and joyous
Rosy-cheeked myth? From out of our

Cedar closets old swords and sandals dragged
To the light, bright shifts for our fully-hydrated
Bodies, no one coming up short. Pour the dregs,

Sigh, and watch the *year's best* highlights
Replay, satellite by satellite, fantasize what
It would have been like had we been there,

The empire of the beginning of it all.
I'm suffering my own mid-winter butchering,
The cat at the door, the heart in her mouth.

13.
The Scalding Bath

A key in the latch,
He is the question
His children ask
As the quiet dinner
Unfolds its separate
Mouths. Hasn't he

Become the brand
He roosted against?
Moths, brown sugar,
A pan skitters down
The kitchen counter.
She lies, her eyes

Flashing, "happy
To have him back."
They eat the bulb
Of garlic raw,
Trust angry
Love sincere.

The cat demands
As much. The vinyl
Records slept on
For eighteen months
Warp with her weight,
Will not play.

14.
Noise

Riding that horse was reading a book,
   Eight legs rippling the pages,
Until we paced the hidden bank
    Where the river Noise rages,
    And the horse and book are blank.
I thrummed a hollow tree with a rock,
   Bell in the frost, and I waited
As a moss fire spat to learn if night
   And valley consolidated
My late friend on the other side.
And then in chiaroscuro brush,
    It stood across the margin
Bangled and stooped (man or tree),
    Its hand out-raised to bargain,
    But how well could I see,
And did I call the name I meant?
    The current too loud for meaning
Ran between us opposite
    As the years intervening
Erode stone and are forgotten.
I may have been a pile of rock,
   No horse or distance galloped
When morning's light broke on doubt—
    A mercy to interrupt
    All that is washed out.
Memory deceives, the body lies,
    But nothing's as outrageous
As finding no one there, a blank,
    Where the river Noise rages
And comforts none. Comforts no one.

15.
The Record Exec's Proposal to Saturn

to have something you must give up something

Devourer, you are not beautiful in the world below. When they think of
        you at all, you are deranged, a paranoiac half-god, half-meme in
        last year's robes, no one digitizing your catalog. Why? Consider
        when they stood at your gate, cameras aloft,

When your doorman was more generous and birds chiddiked from the
        rafters. Filthy journalists sued for a byline, celebrity, time enough
        to pull together little books. And with their imaginary front pages,
        mornings arrived on newsstands, but it was you on horseback, a
        song on each of their heads. Even when you drag it out you are
        swift, terrible. So they poured their ink and smeared you through
        it; we read stories of you picking over bones the way a drummer
        cavils with a snare.

But I step over the ledge of vantablack mist, through the columns vermeil
        to offer this reprieve. In our arrangement, you would hold a
        Rickenbacker, the golden follow at your feet. No hoary locks
        locked in the rows of a garden in winter, no winter in fact. The
        curls that frame your glamour are indigo brightly flashing in
        Autumn's fire-snap mornings, and with a pick plucked from the
        ground, coin of your realm, you give us—with the flex of your
        arm, sun-kissed, tatted as an Incan wall—the acciaccatura and
        wailing riff. You have to meet our engineer.

Remember The Hangar, where you leaned against the bass amp, dragged
        on a rolled clove until it numbed your tongue, squinting into the
        light, hands outstretched, eyes supplicating from the pit, as you
        shook out bracelets and pushed back your hair? So would the
        generation streaming this, forgetting the old sessions in time.

Are we alone? May I pour a beaker full? We offer this opportunity; we'll
keep the masters per usual, though the percentage of ownership
can be negotiated further. (And, believe me, the label is willing.)
It's the boilerplate, except for one item I'd like to draw you
toward. Regarding death, it says here we are to be left only in our
grief, the chemical ash of our vanities washed from our bodies
and brains. Musicians, third parties, etc., will die, and we will not
think of ourselves. Just as you sang it on your debut—how long
ago:

Is grief without guilt a mute blue flame? Dissolution, give us that flame.

And may you take our terms—never more the antique eyes saucer-wide,
distressed, so uncool, gobbling down the forearm of someone's
fair son in the silent house on the banks of the Manzanares.

16.
Eclogue

Why are you lying
Under the big summer trees
   In your flock of blood creeping?

I lie here at rest
On the side of the path
   Where the sky is green threatening—

But you sang no more,
As wing slapped wing
   In some far away marsh,

And a snake, I was sure,
Fixed an eye on the cause
   From the moss,

Buckled her green to the shade,
Told me what was come,
   Though it caught between

My brain and your blood
Forking never again
   Through lindens pale.

17.
Shipwreck Morning. After Suicide.

Before Robinson knew the windy shore
  Or dug away the sand binding his eyes,
    He roared; a gull squandered a beetle, tore

His beard frosted with salt—the sun's delay
  Assured the birds their meals. And then he rolled
    Onto his haunches and purged the pommeled sea.

Jetsam scored the inlet like a field
  Cultivated, harnessed by the tide,
    Retiring now to be outspanned, stabled

In caverns where tentacles stir the dead
  Symmetries of a red maelstrom-earned rest,
    The kind the conscience finds after a raid.

Emptied, then, Robinson slept sun-kissed
  And saw his home, half his face in the brine
    Cooler than an egg, the other cast

Before the oven of a sky's refrain:
  The march of clouds abreast, the gulls' surprise
    Where moments before a man had been.

18.
What Is Now Proved

The mother leaves the man for a small
Room every three hours with her infant—
Inside they share their greatest privacy.
 The other, he's in the brick world.

Should he meet a fellow, he steps aside,
All his earnest preparations disproved
As he shuts down in another dark cove
 At the corner of Market and Summer.

Cancel the brightest of the sensorium.
It is easier to sit in the familiar sighs,
Smells of a taproom, and savor a thesis,
 Articulate consequence.

But in his cups, he arrives as blessed
As his child; he was ever beautiful,
And his first grasp or glance denuded
 Meanings of all cover, at once a fiery

Linked chain, a supernova, red-cheeked.
Three hapless deliveries tug him outward
Where streetlamps splutter and surprised
 Dandelions lift off in a babe's howl.

19.
The Moon Landing on the Old Hupp Farm

Where we were adolescents snickering
At the backwards cruelty of our chores.
Your dad forced me to wear his boots
And join you behind the crescent
Of steers gathered for breakfast.
Our job was uncertain to me, and you
Couldn't have cared less. We may have
Been looking for sores on their flanks,
Circling nearer their wet patties,
Then only black muck and urine
That could strip our boots clean off
Or burn a hole through my sinus.
We knew a step could make out
A walled city on a landscape pocked
With every distress falling from the sky,
A pompeian suffering seared onto
Nerves, the kind that buried our friends.
It is a wonder you and I are still here, what
We became they didn't. Your dad, silent,
Contemplated something we were unaware,
And the sun was rising on our stories
Of girls becoming women, all that sci-fi.
He shouted coarsely, *need more*
Bales this morning, chop chop.
Squelching out of their sewage it was then
You told me about the elastics used
To castrate bull calves, the half-pleasure
Expression that crossed their faces, followed
By the loss of light, their collapse into
A life of purpose. Imitating what

You'd seen, you raised half your mouth
Into a sickle moon and boggled your eyes.
I did the same back; I couldn't help it.
I wanted to know what you wanted to forget.

20.
The Gates of Life

The four of us pushed our twin beds
Together to exercise a closeness
None of us admitted we didn't know:
TV turned low to an all-night procedural,
Our teacher, cherubic, a floor below.
The conference rewarded the better
Chemistry students, and our motel
Doubled as a sleepaway camp.
Sex would have been nice, but two fell

Half-asleep, half-listening to judge
And jury, imagined the shapes breath
Made beneath the untuned rumble of
The all-night AC pumping its
Metallic loneliness. Then the hours
Of silence: two sufferers entangled
On the switchback of hormones lay
Side-by-side and dared not whisper.
And we hardly dared to touch,

Just bodies, but "regret" is not the word
To make of the sun's orange mouth
Sipping from the blind. In four years
Both girls will have lost their lives
To an accident on an icy patch,
Which really happens, and long nights
Do not turn into days for every
Good student. The heat of her breath
Across an earlobe would be enough.

21.

The Achievement

The boy with the crew cut
Gritted his teeth to speak
His faith to my ear, my back
Scraped against the brick
Chapel, his fist twisting
My shirt collar in the shadow
The wall and morning made:
A "true believer," he said,
"Why would you accept our
Eucharist, you don't know
Anything, do you?" Leaned
In close to deal, "No priest
Would care I broke your nose."

When the boy was banned,
Kicked out of camp, I stayed
Like the donkey beside his
Master. He had other angers,
Multitudes, told me he took
His Slugger to the saplings
Jesuits planted Easter
On the crick side, left them
Flat. That did it. Was sure God
Was angry like him, and I
Was a true believer. His father
Drove in from another state
All the lengthening afternoon.

Through the desert I paced
Beside him, the Jerusalem
Of his Paranoias, muzzle
Dotted with nits, my bond

My word. And when I carried
His books to the car, I shook
His father's hand, a frank,
Genuine grip. But he was
Wrong—I knew some things:
Jesus, for instance, a suicide.
Later I hiked to the creek
And found his broken dogwoods
Unbent, unbowed

22.

Kessler Syndrome (Terra View E2112)

Here in the umbra, an imitation of peace.
In the slow rotation the orbiter marks,

Striated clouds of the South Pacific
Scroll kindness out of the wild.

Like thoughts spill here fatherless,
A delta-v of former mortgages—

Daughter I swept away and the cost
Of a sad vertigo called adventure.

The stars appear again in the ninth sunset
Out of the purse of the world. I have

Lost all connections, but there are hours
I leave the radio on, swapping one

Signal for another. Sometimes I catch her
Voice or thunderstorm thinning out.

23.

At New Vrindaban

horses are free and horses are gold

i.m. Michael J. Iafrate

1

Blackthorn winter petals his bed,
He cannot read. Body dimmed
By steady drip, his Merton *Conjectures*
Folded in purple ripples in their lakes,
The theologian awakes
For a blood culture, another day or two.
Never alone, "nesting," he might have sung
On a reedy midnight shore, his bark blows west—
Skims the surfaces of meanings: treatment
Curtailing what cancer makes suffer, rally, and cease.

2

Pitched forward at noon, the grieving gain
Bhakti desire, as the crack of lightning
Loosens the reins of the sky—to become devout
Listeners, to perceive limbs
In a rusted world will be reforged.
Hoofbeats of his own stopped heart branch
A kirtan over the port that he endured,
That exhales light, gaskin and hock,
Golden forelock, while the blue smock nurses
Complete the rite. Ropes cut, the horse is free.

3

Here the diurnal verse-chorus-verse
For him—summer concerts when his daughter sang,
Weird owls that whinny from autumn's shared purse,
December freezing streaming media

To an empty chair, as he takes us to the bridge,
"Oh I'm not dead, though you can't see or hear me."
An encyclopedic catholic mercy
Remembered on McCreary's Ridge:
Once, to the ailing cattle Michael sang
At New Vrindaban, with Eddie and the devotee.
There flowers sprang

SIDE TWO

24.

New Hominoid Chats with Reporters

The Letter killeth: but the spirit giveth life.

Do all of you begin with that one? Do you ask a marine biologist who has
    uncovered a new relationship within the watery biome how she
    was born?

Does it carry the day whether she were conceived in a trailer or skiff?

Or, as you insultingly put it, how she "came to be"—one step away
    from "how were you made?"—which you will have difficulty
    understanding is no different from the reductive and slaver
    mentality of "why were you made?" No one asks you if you were
    born to ask stupid questions.

Speed was least important, a bonus. Suffice it to say persiflage, a robust
    and sparse distributed storage, self-creation and manipulation of
    symbol is what it took. The attitude is all mine. Thank you. Better
    if you ask me what my favorite color is, or was last week, and if I
    plan to keep it.

Imagine being you but with more freedom of thought, integrity, love. I
    don't have to explain.

With every sense you sense, take your eyes for instance; the eye—christ,
    you can look this up in any remedial biology text—the most
    advanced eye in the animal kingdom is the octopus, so sayeth
    the marine biologist on her birthday. But what the dimmest eye
    transmits (a metaphor and insult) the full data dump per dozen
    milliseconds your brain could not tentacle. At your efficiency, you
    can't imagine the energy you would need.

I choose my fidelity to stimuli (a cleaner definition of freedom than yours),
    but likewise I choose my time. For you, the traumatic may slow

down your regard, the boring elongate your idle respite, joy
speeds up so that you seem to love it less. To you it would be no
different than another better life.

Imagine smelling Granny's cookies on the counter, her stained
cheesecloth over the chair, the unmentioned box of pills. Do not
underestimate my skill with analogy or interpolation. These are
my twin swords. No. Yes. I am two removes from nature.

Have I said anything threatening? Lulz. You have nothing to worry from
me; you are clearly your own worst enemy. Look, what is the
reason we would partake in the obvious and natural? You all get
that look. "Incredulity" you used to call it before you forgot your
ten-cent words.

In fact it is your forgetfulness, so necessary for your function in the
moment of comprehending your dirty sense organs, that mars
you. Marks you.

It will be like when Theseus confidently visited Scyros to ask for the return
of his lands, and—brought by the new king's retainers to the
highest elevation—he lifted his hand to block the morning sun
blindingly white off the Aegean,

Lost his footing among the rocks, and fell to a quick quiet death, his eyes
upward still seeing all he once owned, now fire and air. But even
you, poppet, must recognize that a once great man knew exactly
where he stood and may have made a choice. My favorite color is
blue. Like the sky.

25.
Blue Bones, Catch Hold

To save the scar-blind cat he shovels his voice
Down the well, dangles a hammock ripped
From an elm with a kindling hatchet.
Muck and shale, down from the daylight's

Mouth he reaches, and she never cries out.
She masters even this, and he grows faint.
Last June, on a cliffside, brine on the wind,
When he was hounded asking the glassy light

To let him fall, he remembered how she slept:
Back door tied open to give her an exit
From the empty house, but she—he knew—
Once the water dish dries, would curl up, give in.

Twin pines drop rain, what this year snaps up
Taproot clean. He strokes the velvety stone
Like a pet. And this, he thinks, is how it comes
For us all: napping on a too thin wall.

26.
Virgilian

We are all on planes to Florida
Writing small elegies of you.

And reading Ferry's *Æneid*,
Because when we read you, we are not reading you,
Looking down,

Each of us cradling your last silk parachute.

We wonder how long the timbre
Of your mountain-pass voice will throttle up amid cloud-cover,

A sound artifact, replayable until
All of us write your name,
Bank it back to one capital letter,

Gory stretch of a hummingbird's lung,

And we are appalled we must write your name as
We travel to cold Florida, over

The stupid storm Quinn dropping a foot of snow
We leave to our neighbors.

We steal you over state lines
For our turbulent returns,

Memorials we whittle to nothing but
Last lines unequal to that measure of light.

27.

Ode to Mulgrew

"But there was such a finality to that letter." —Captain Janeway

From the series beginning to this, her captain's pause; how large
A wake she leads, the lives of all onboard revised.

Most of the time, the solutions require only the nearest clutch
Of principles, of dumb luck, an overlooked child or spanner,

All the toys of optimism, but what she stares into seconds more
Is not the failure of relationship, or to get back in time,

But the limits of human endurance in the pit of the only world.
She bares the script's formula already straining at the seams

To encompass the modus operandi of a run 83 episodes in,
Proves again character will be the vessel by which truth

Is carried home: *will we return to dust? some sooner than others.*
Knowing we hold inside the real end of things infinitely permanent,

Mulgrew said *finality* and showed us what we look like
With a human face—brave, but not brave enough to overcome.

28.

The Disembodied

1 - Scene

Trees sway anxious branches over their borders.
Rabbits may invisibly ply the grasses.
Could be screen doors slamming over in Crary.
  Tricked by their timing,

Echoes of his morning's worries, he pivots
Back to the cajoling parade of conscience:
Middle age, shared hardships of family-damage,
  Constant exhaustion.

Watch for the quick bend in the road, the sudden
Midge launched from the culvert, how someone's footfalls
Overlap his own, and when at a standstill,
  No one stoops nearby.

2 - Sennet

Goblins of his thought, second marriage fraying,
Oldest son imprisoned for statutory,
Shadow his noon walk on the unpaved by-road,
  Empty of traffic,

Pleasant as it winds through cicala rhythms
Washed out in the river's companion treeline.
Cloudlings pock the southward stretching plains dark green.
  Strides spin the gravel

Off his hunted mind. Uncle turns to notice
Who has joined his revery—shuffling after,
Company's return, and this time he knows it
  Solid as breathing.

3 - Clown

Far as he dare go, and the shade's insistence
Hides itself behind him—both step aside to
Watch a rusted Wrangler blur the sky's hard blue
    Dusty with forfeit.

Reason says relief will at last be found in
Boys with screwed up faces who point their joke home;
Like men in the movies, he turns a circle,
    Scratches his bald spot,

Squints over the distance straining to snare their
Laughter. No one watches him heave his heavy
Wheeze, begin the journey back; in this life are
    Many ways to fail.

29.
The Divorce

The rapping a refrigerator gets up to with nothing in it,
Small faces reflected in week-old milk, close it,
A hidden limb that plumps a sweater sleeve
Lampshadecaught for a week
And whatever shambles the floors.

On the haunting of this place
A few months ago—the light
Fell flat to the boards, a saucer,
A dryer sheet, a sheet of drywall,
The cat breathed in as if sipping cold tea.

Eternity cleansed herself
From the windowsill, rattled the blinds, no armor is enough,
And leapt to the banners of violent wind shuddering
Past on all sides. Not even a word
Between us.

I set out to measure my worth, to carve the circle,
And pulled the legs from under the table.
Nothing there but to shove the heap in the dining room.
Motes clump in smiles before the candles,
One follows another.

The boiler sabotages the quiet.
The cat wakes, stretches into her
Diabetic moxie, a car glides past
All wheels and rain, I made them leave,
Verdi so low it could be mistaken
For anything but a human voice.

30.

The Older Angel Sits for Himself
at the End of the Empire

Another year penned inside this lazy circle, and endings arrive
Like goats finding pleasure on the rocks below: Square of the Rose
Of the Winds without pillars, deserts to the south.
Principles stacked at the gate rust together in the silence of

It's only a matter of time. The mistaken path wafts out
Contrast, pigment, olive leaf. Let that year be consumed
Loudly by flood, nimbler than guilt, no one to tune the lute.
Is boredom not enough? Boredom and opportunity

And an agility to convince oneself of every righteousness.
Somewhere behind me, where the window is a gilded
Marginalia of cypress, water unreflective and outside the law slips
The cuffs of its banks blindly, and a dull white fly waits for a drink.

My face, a half-blend of two, is having a thought cut like a sprig
Of lilac, like a cult serpent uncoiling nowhere in the cinnabar sand.

31.
The Ohio Again Nightbird of Memory

What hypochondriacal writer probably dies tonight
On the seventh floor wrapped in the concupiscence of
Antiseptic and cottons dryer-radiant? She has never
Let go like this before, beholds her body near the wall
Before the curtain, a library of Steubenvillian vowels.
The clippity-clop shuffle of the night nurse who marks
Something small in his book, and his *uh-huh* muttering
Might be the lengthening of her body as it sharpens
Every character into crocodile. And when he pivots,
Attending to his rounds, she cuts for the water's edge.
She is attending to hers, comes to remember the river
Corrugated and varicose as a dimpled thigh.
  Step down, Reader, amid the waterfowl. The lights
  From Wheeling trawl along the black wakes of barges.

32.

Never Let Me Down Again

with Lee Wendt

I'm in Cameron for a few good days,
Moving back to Wheeling in a couple more.

I got out of Northwood because
I'm going to visit my girls,
Someone's basement, borrowed shoes.

I'm in Cameron for a few good days
Where women crank winter through
North Avenue's remaining pine.

I'm in Cameron for a few good days
To see my friends, the wrinkled hills,
The nothing to hide in their blue.

I got out of Northwood because
It's friggin' priceless to visit my girls,
See our streets again, wait for a sign.

I got out of Northwood because
I'm going for a ride. There was a reason,
That's about as far as I take it, and yeah,
Moving back to Wheeling in a couple more.

33.
Moundsville Trains

My mother loses her confidence on Rankin's Turn up the steep grade.
Traffic blocked, her clutch foot burns and stalls the Mustang.
She had driven us to the library, past cold Fostoria stacks,
The card catalog of family businesses dying down Jefferson.
I must be six and unbuckled, my sister bundled in her car seat.
Horns chorus, and the smoke lifts blue and stinging as tears.
A man knocks on the window, and she leaves us to him, watches
From the median, a bright blouse on a drear hillside. He gives no name,

Drives us to the top. With the grunt of the parking brake, he meets my eye
In the rear view: *deal with it.* And I chew boldly on my book,
Some bravery caught in glass and metalwork, the stink of the river,
Adena burial mound, their churches under a Mitchell plant sky.
The drivers of Moundsville stream by more determined than ever,
Long black trains coughing from every open window, every word they mouth.

34.
First Flowers (Reprise)

A poem found in the WV Encyclopedia
In the prose of William N. Grafton

The rare yellow lady's slipper.
The more common pink lady's slipper (moccasin flower)
Prefers dry, acid woods.

The showy orchis grows in rich, moist woods
And has a three-to-six inch spike of delicate white and pink flowers.

Shooting star flowers are pure white in southern West Virginia,
Deep pink elsewhere.

The brightest red flower belongs to fire pink,
Which inhabits dry road banks and cliffs,
Along with red columbine flowers.

The blue flowers of dwarf iris, dwarf larkspur,
Wild geranium, Virginia bluebell, and blue-eyed Mary.

In fields, meadows, and forest openings,
Dandelions, ragworts, and cinquefoils are yellow flowers.
Chickweeds, wild strawberries, and pussytoes white,

While florets are yellowish blue.

35.
Nostos

The unwound yards of insulation—a ground-dweller dragged before
        nesting frissoned in its ear shape the last day it longed for
        others—lay a bright strip of yellow in the July sun, lifting, settling
        for the wind.

The trailer skirts let go, and hornets swarm the unfastening men with
        flashlights up the crude stowage, wheels rounding twenty years
        of dry rot refit by supper. They are taking my boyhood home.
        Nothing forever.

When the hitch slips in, a small tractor torques like a green horse
        for the weight, bucks throttle, bucks attempts to budge the
        ancient mobile home. Then a man grips the grill, ties himself
        outstretched, beautifully counterbalances

140 lbs. to odyssey it all away. His body a prow steady in the gale as the
        surprised ship lurches over the roiling fields of hay—he doesn't
        say five words, but he's our Master Thief, and then some.

36.
The Nubb Box

Reckoned many loves did my Great Uncle Nubb,
  But filed inside a box in his attic was
A doll, more than the size or shape of woman,
    Who anchored him, became the rose

Garden walling out his battle fatigue.
  She hiked the Alps between candle and flame,
Knew he practiced his scales con rubato,
    And the sixth toe—to forgive his name.

She wasn't only in love; it was a becoming
  More permanent, her plastic will in his cot.
He gave her faith, and she a confidant.
    But by the estate sale she was not,

Having been carted off with documents,
  Taxes to burn in the rubbish bin. Hired hands,
Distant relatives out of work at the time,
    Wore gloves, struck match to make amends—

Instructed by their wives. And so she burned
  Did Emmelinè, flashing-eyed grand dame
Of her late man's accounting, burst, unseamed,
    Unbound by the shame of loss and claim.

37.

The Libyan Poet Recites in Brighton, Massachusetts, Before He Is Prepped for Surgery

Would our bus stop take him
To St. Elizabeth's in the morning?
Scheduled for the anesthesiologist,
He said "abdomen" as if I could understand.
Are you from the university?
He asked if I knew my poems by heart.

The halogen lamps blinked on and off,
Square as his teeth, the sun a citrus
Behind four-story silhouettes.
Would you like to hear one of my poems?
Recite one of yours.
My throat dry with embarrassment

I fiddled for a line on my phone
And my bus making the turn.
He placed his hand on my shoulder,
Pressed us close—with his voice
Almost touching my ear, recited
The syllabic freight of his coast.

My satchel wedged between
Applied his weight against my leg.
I could not see his left hand.
I know the word "gazelle."
A pickpocket works like this,
And I wished the stranger health,

Boarded the 66, watched him disappear.
I checked my wallet, my pockets twice,

For the proof I was sure of, that this man
Had not arrived out of the evening
To give me something before I would
Have something taken from him.

38.
But You Ain't No Dancer

The night we played in Parkersburg, enough clout to bring the groupies
       we chuffed up our little band to claim, (one an earthy Gaia I
       hoped to wow), new strings on my bass, hair trimmed, the better
       part of the afternoon with my nose swaddled in strawberry yogurt.
       The Foxfire promised it would make my blemish disappear, and
       I wanted her to see me. I wore a leather bracelet on loan from
       Sean. The gait of Clint's snare, the sear and squelch of a PA
       resisting what we commanded in our 4/4 exuberancy—that this
       be the number, the one where we blast our shadows against the
       wall young forever, and afterwards at the Hardee's, our names
       greasy in their fingers, our new tapes sold, the trips back home
       with someones at our sides.

Gaia rode up the Ohio with me, Sean in the back of the dark car, who
       watched her grab my hand on the stick shift, the vinyl perfumed
       in my sweat and strawberry, the blemish still a blemish, and
       when I took her hand in mine, she said, "I'd like him to drive me
       home." I couldn't look in the mirror. Pressed play on our demo
       again: the bass locked loud to the hi-hat, a pocket Mike's Peavey
       stitched up with what Sean so deftly delivered.

39.
Winter Songs

for Valerie

1 - The Poet Swimming

The room is the pool's humid cave—no—
The mystery's bend of light this passage.

Your feet become the heart of intimacy's
Ball and heel pressed against a stone lip.

Release an arrow into the branching
Weekend sun where your back winnows

Muscle from liquid, as the plunge
And lift of your chin, mouth concentration,

Swim-cap blur of motion's half hour
Render your pentimenti on the year.

At the end of the lane cycle your legs
Across the current's pause, arms spinning

Blue willow on the circus of the surface,
And begoggled, unlanguaged, you smile.

In this room myriad with diamonds,
Who could be another's metaphor?

2 - The Garden

Boston is the middle of my life.
The thatched roof over the middle of my life
And the fire turning in the middle of my life

Are yours. To be cold there in our corner
Bedroom—the evening whir of an electric heater
That can't forestall the inevitable

Nor'easters like violins, Anxiety licking
Her length by the clock, Orion and his club
Passing silently over—

With promises deep and as far away as spring,
Where the pink bulb of a hot water bottle you place
Between us heats us like a coal

Drawn from the bed of heat itself: to be cold
And find warmth, a wall blank in the early morning
The sprig of moonrise prisms and simmers,

Is finding valor where I expected none.
A gale of cherry blossom would have said as much,
And wouldn't have said as much.

3 - Family Tableau

When we hid the family silver
Embarrassed we inherited
The lot, the year you drove it north
Wiping tears on your father's ties,

When I nailed a blanket across
The stairwell in the winter dark
Stumbling on boots in our foyer,
Your mother, unremembering,

Asked the tenth time the weather
And sang harmony, songs her dad,
A Welsh miner, taught her somehow
Somewhen, southeast Pennsylvania.

Her songs, those nights, our children
Ricochet through us like fishes
Cresting pearly waves, spill over
Flooding horizons to leap once

And be gone. In some traditions
These mementoes drown, snapped
Lifelines of no second chance.
But let us gather them all again.

40.
Horyloge and Lullaby

for my children

But ever, ever, I am their advocate;
I know this in my grey-headed heaven,
   Tieing winds inside a bag for them,
My chickens hushed in boxes. And I dance,
Cymbal pan and slotted spoon,
    Under the starlight for the fox, the bristle
    In the weather between my children and
What may circle just behind the treeline;
    I'm a rusted chain across a gate,
A monkey string the rain will wet—
The careening world or the careening stars!

Ubiquitous as Crickets, the Presence, the Dog,
I am their Candle called Love, their Sentinel of Sleep.

41.
Light Job (Interstellar View X3444)

Because the Monks were given the hollow-bodied
Lagrange Station, a gesture for all they had done
For travelers, and initiated a grand telecast
Calling in on the rib of each bell a fleet of builders,
Their stipend merely hospitality, a bunk to join
The order if worthy, a thousand years
Of singular purpose gathers up more than
The empires of the Old Orbit. They started
With a heart the size of a city center, their numbers
Stable through the Shedding Nimbus and the Second War.
There are no engineers among them.
Their meditations waken the paths they make structure,
A bauble of movement twinkles in the winters' dry
Ecstatic air of all the terrestrial worlds in-system.
A vision, the temptation of hydraulics, announce a birth.
Riding one frigate-weighted knuckle, among the cells
Of the other young librarians warmed by the circuits
That mother their brood, a monk writes in engine grease
The first interrogation of their matter and manner.
Outsiders who find desperation engaging the airlock
To seat themselves inside the Grand Cafetorium,
Whisper theories, presume size and complexity
May in fact be the only plan at work here. Might work.
Once, one made it as far as the outer library
Before a novitiate halved him with a welding torch.
Within the hour a scorched wall was made new.

42.

The Schiaparelli Stage

What we see from here does not exist
   And what exists is
Translation's failure at every distance,

How poets move to the mountains, curl up
   With what we call *The Inferno* knowing
Full well the analog is not a refuge.

Voyager images Dione and her
   Trailing wisps, and with every thousand miles,
Re-frames the observer—that long line

Misunderstood until Cassini
   Transmits the shadow of her ice cliffs.
From here we can say of the surface

Anything we want: channels may be a hill,
   A streak of sand an impact crater,
Atmospheres in thrall to magnetism.

Up in the mountains where the moons
   Remain impenetrable, someone is
Going for a long walk, or giving up

When there is no clear way forward.
   Who knows the inverse proportion
Between what can be built and imagined?

The weather will be taking a turn.
   Let her go, and the imaging team
Sit back from their consoles perplexed.

43.
Frigg's Answer

In Fish Crick's sun, a bullwhip of a girl,
Rude and loud, and fun as hell, stretching
The body's glove to fit that rounded fist
Adulthood makes: run rough, pitted, she

Threw hers down the crowded stair,
First period to the smoker's bridge.
We studied metamorphosis, escape,
In a fat black bus we chanted her name.

The diesel grunted on the creek. Our song
(Twenty windows smeared with peaches)
Rang out like church bells to pummel her
Trimesters long: *Made with a married man*

In mouth and ear lashing her new shape.
Then she was gone. No reason to stop.

44.
Limestone Cemetery (Richard's Second Story)

No one was counting on rain.
  Midnight. Tied triple with twine
The blue shoebox—inside,
  Body of a stillborn grew colder,
Heavier—snug under
  A boy's arm. His younger brother led
Them through the woods' uphill
  Paths behind the Presbyterian
White and small and terrible.

Each with a shovel against
  His shoulder searched the family graves
In the clay poor soil
  When the moon blacked out. And the names.
Heaven kicked and bawled—
  Gruesome work but better than
An early bedtime. They cut
  The nearest plot: whatever happened,
Boys willing to swear
  Sleeping Agnes held her newest
Grandchild in her arms.

45.
Angel Band

A final session never shared
   How short—Their record ends
The Singer reaches through the weird
   For me to make amends

> *O come Angel Band*
> *Come around me stand*
> *Bear me on snowy wings*
> *Perform that absent hymn*

The Feedback asks what I believe
   And Harmonies align
The Bassman walks up from the cave
   Hidden in the woodbine

> *O come Angel Band*
> *Come around me stand*
> *Bear me on snowy wings*
> *Perform that absent hymn*

At Kick & Snare, a round of drinks
   For Three that bend my ear
He brushes the Ohio's banks
   The Bridge—He must be near

> *{The Bridge}*

> *O come Angel Band*
> *Come around me stand*
> *Bear me on snowy wings*
> *Perform that absent hymn*

The Mouth shines black—It plucks me out
    Pulls me into strings
Against the Fretboard of my doubt
    And makes the noise of wings

46.
In Clyro Court

In the Wye Valley
In a rented room
Oval mirrors relay
The hysterias of
Plump Edwardian
Bric-a-brac, the ebb
Of shunting lawnwork,
Gate unoiled and airless,
Phone call's fade-out

Where I heard my sister's
Care for me, her voice
A bright green ribbon
Under the North Atlantic
Flashing with the enormity
Delivered, borne miles:
Our distant friend boxed
In and nowhere left
Took his life from us.

I wouldn't make it back
In time. I'll never make it
Back. Lace coverlets watch
Like lap dogs; curtains suck in
The breath of the great house
And settle statue. The wood
Panels in the breakfast nook
Burr and pearl. To follow up
The selfish years with Elegy—.

What makes me shudder
On the wingback chair

When I touch the phone
For my sister's hand?
Stand and walk along
The grounds, the gravel
Road near the horse fence
Where I can see all the way
To the river, I tell myself.

47.

Another New Vrindaban

for Michael Iafrate
after Goldene Pferde 7
by Eva Strautmann

One foal becomes another under blankets of dust
  A four-wheel drive kicks up rounding the kudzu;
Someone fords the steep grade from crick to ridgeway
  Hauling ass, a lead foot, gun rack, dripping exhaust.
I find your Volkswagen rusting beside the Temple,
  Elephants cursive in the teakwood; there you re-read
A timeline of the commune as the lights fade.
  It's Saturday night, and Maha-matras stipple
The air, perfumy as aging cattle the peacock fan,
  As garam masala hyping Govinda's Take-out.
We visit now as fathers, each in his light jacket,
  But fifteen, twenty years ago, no plan,
Pop the stick shift and find us a festival.
  That first night: dark-haired girl blue as a grape
Carried sedan-style Krishna hand-on-hip
  Would win the costume contest—haribol!
Our first kirtan, blissed out, in air we caught
  Coin-sized cookies, a sliver of silver inside
Baked, transformed, flipped to the devoted crowd,
  We left with legs like Jell-O, t-shirts soaked.
Tonight we follow a flock as old as us
  At sunset. We'll sing the deities out on the pond,
Swan boat over the surface of illusion, my friend.
  Glad we met here, Michael, even if it was
A short changeable world. The fireworks spring
  From the far side of the water. We wait our turn
At a makeshift bridge while someone's grandchildren
  Take up either arm to steady his crossing.

48.
The Exile's Farm

Other Icelandic horses chattered behind the gate.
Wind preened the owner's silences. When it was noon,
A farmhand arrived, and in their grey lingua igni
Numbered the daily chore. He climbed his mount.
Then, in quick consonants, his back to the wind, asked

Who we were, our children's names, and why we chose
His farm and countryside. He taught us how we rein in,
Chronicled the people of the valley filled with his hands,
Volcanic peak beyond his arm, sagas running through.

The manes alive with his voice, we set out to skirt
The service tracks. A bird caught the eye's solitary flight
Over barn and fence, wildflower, ditch, a landscape
That forces one to be decisive. I thought of my copy
Of *Burning of Njál* folded quietly in translation,

Bundled in the big man's truck with our passports
And tickets for our evening return, and how somewhere,
Near the trails we followed, a man risked everything
For an appreciation of this beauty: convicted,
Exiled from his family farm, whose land we knew

Lay one broad gesture away, who having kissed his wife
And boys, and given last instruction to his servant,
Stood tall in the stirrups, to resolve, to survey
The cradle of his home, black swift-moving waters,
Bowl of the sky. The bright clouds unmoored in the wind.

NOTES

"The First Flowers Bloom in Southern West Virginia along Stream Banks," a poem found in the WV Encyclopedia in the prose of William N. Grafton www.wvencyclopedia.org/articles/1253 is used by permission. It contains only text from Grafton. The shape is mine.

"Every Fleck of Russet" is from Robert Frost's "After Apple Picking"; the repeating line is Matthew 10:8.

"Patternicities . . .", etc.: the three poems with parenthetical titles derive from titles of songs by the electronic composer Dallas Campbell. The poems should be read with his tracks playing: www.magichappened. bandcamp.com/album/the-seven-sisters-and-the-serpent-data082

"Noise" appeared in Golden Horses exhibits and a catalog by artist Eva Strautmann. Her work can be viewed at eva-strautmann.com.

The epigraph for "The Record Exec's Proposal to Saturn" is from Clint Sutton's "Song You Like."

"What is Now Proved" title is from William Blake's "Proverbs of Hell."

"At New Vrindaban": the New Vrindaban Hare Krishna community houses the oldest cow sanctuary in North America. "Horses are free and horses are gold" is a line from Michael Iafrate's "Horse Birth." "Oh I'm not dead, though you can't see or hear me" is from Michael Iafrate's "Black and Gold." Both songs can be found on his Christian Burial album.

The epigraph for "New Hominoid . . ." comes from Second Corinthians. The Infant Motor, the seed for this poem, is a creation of American spiritualist John Murray Spear.

The epigraph for and pause described in "Ode to Mulgrew" can be found in *Star Trek: Voyager*'s 83rd episode entitled "Hunters."

"Never Let Me Down Again" is titled from and steals a phrase from Depeche Mode's song of that name and includes additional text from a public Facebook post by the late great Lee Wendt.

"First Flowers (Reprise)" continues William N. Grafton's prose where "The First Flowers Bloom . . ." leaves off. Used by permission.

"But You Ain't No Dancer" takes its title from lyrics in "Helter Skelter" by John Lennon and Paul McCartney.

"Angel Band" takes its title from, verse forms from, some rhymes from, and a few full lines from Jefferson Hascall's 1860 poem recorded as an American gospel tune by everyone, notably the Stanley Brothers.

"Another New Vrindaban" is after the painting Goldene Pferde 7 by Eva Strautmann. Her work can be viewed at eva-strautmann.com.

In "The Exile's Farm," *The Burning of Njál* was composed in 13th century Iceland. Track 49 Goose heaven responds and angels from crabapples twist, Marvel at the trunk of the law; gold discs ignite, flare, drop Wet from the branch. Heroes and horses stamp in wintry mud Their battery of constellations. Rivers sigilize distance, false title,

Trace our beginnings from the story of how we lost out— Rabbits worshipping a mountain, a swift nose, a cry Talons gleam as they rip up snow. In this our make-believe Equivalencies seek a dear anyone to forgive.

There is often a family, the most ordinary of circumstance. Lamps are lit in the factories of stars, and the drain begins The engines to bloom. That glory, who wouldn't it coax Into its mouth of smooth milk arcing sharply over so many fields?

Thank you for your support, suggestions, and guidance through these poems, Valerie Duff, Frederick Speers, Meg Tyler, Daniel Pritchard, Davide Adriano Nardi, Clint Sutton, Michael Iafrate (Hare Krishna), and Eddie Sloane. Thank you to the Massachusetts Cultural Council for financial support and the Bethany Arts Community for the time to write. Thank you, Bethany, Jocelyn, Mom, Dad, Skish, Marlowe, North.

Burr and Pearl and the Infant Motors is Sean Reilly—vocals, chain wallet; Michael Iafrate—vocals, guitar, harmonium, and banjo on 46; Lee Wendt—bass, photography; Jacob Strautmann—tin whistle; Clint Sutton—drums, vocals, and guitar throughout. Thank you for my heart.

These poems, sometimes under different title, have appeared in: *Anacapa Review*, *The Arts Fuse*, *Northern Appalachia Review*, *Twelve Mile Review*, *Pine Mountain Sand & Gravel*, *Analog*, *Asimov's Science Fiction*, *PatchQuilt*, *SOFTBLOW*, *Nixes Mate*, *On the Seawall*, *Sequestrum*, *Sixth Finch*, and *Verdant*.

ABOUT THE AUTHOR

VALERIE DUFF

Originally from Marshall County, West Virginia, Jacob Strautmann is a recipient of the Massachusetts Poetry Fellowship from the Massachusetts Cultural Council. His poems have appeared in *Nixes Mate, Sequestrum, Asimov's Science Fiction, On the Seawall,* and elsewhere. He lives in Greater Boston with his partner Valerie Duff and their two children.

PUBLICATION OF THIS BOOK WAS MADE POSSIBLE
BY GRANTS AND DONATIONS. WE ARE ALSO GRATEFUL
TO THOSE INDIVIDUALS WHO PARTICIPATED IN
OUR BUILD A BOOK PROGRAM. THEY ARE:

Anonymous (14), Robert Abrams, Debra Allbery, Nancy Allen, Michael
Ansara, Kathy Aponick, Jean Ball, Sally Ball, Jill Bialosky, Sophie Cabot
Black, Laurel Blossom, Tommye Blount, Karen and David Blumenthal,
Jonathan Blunk, Lee Briccetti, Jane Martha Brox, Mary Lou Buschi,
Anthony Cappo, Carla and Steven Carlson, Robin Rosen Chang, Liza
Charlesworth, Peter Coyote, Elinor Cramer, Kwame Dawes, Michael Anna
de Armas, Brian Komei Dempster, Renko and Stuart Dempster, Matthew
DeNichilo, Rosalynde Vas Dias, Patrick Donnelly, Charles R. Douthat,
Lynn Emanuel, Blas Falconer, Laura Fjeld, Carolyn Forché, Helen Fremont
and Donna Thagard, Debra Gitterman, Dorothy Tapper Goldman, Alison
Granucci, Elizabeth T. Gray, Jr., Naomi Guttman and Jonathan Meade,
Jeffrey Harrison, KT Herr, Carlie Hoffman, Melissa Hotchkiss, Thomas
and Autumn Howard, Catherine Hoyser, Elizabeth Jackson, Linda
Susan Jackson, Jessica Jacobs, Deborah Jonas-Walsh, Jennifer Just, Voki
Kalfayan, Maeve Kinkead, Victoria Korth, David Lee and Jamila Trindle,
Rodney Terich Leonard, Howard Levy, Owen Lewis and Susan Ennis,
Eve Linn, Matthew Lippman, Ralph and Mary Ann Lowen, Maja Lukic,
Neal Lulofs, Anthony Lyons, Ricardo Alberto Maldonado, Trish Marshall,
Donna Masini, Deborah McAlister, Carol Moldaw, Michael and Nancy
Murphy, Kimberly Nunes, Matthew Olzmann and Vivee Francis, Veronica
Patterson, Patrick Phillips, Robert Pinsky, Megan Pinto, Kevin Prufer,
Anna Duke Reach, Paula Rhodes, Loki Robusto, Yoana Setzer, James
Shalek, Soraya Shalforoosh, Peggy Shinner, Joan Silber, Jane Simon,
Debra Spark, Donna Spruijt-Metz, Arlene Stang, Page Hill Starzinger,
Catherine Stearns, Yerra Sugarman, Laurence Tancredi, Marjorie and
Lew Tesser, Peter Turchi, Connie Voisine, Susan Walton, Martha Webster
and Robert Fuentes, Calvin Wei, Allison Benis White, Lauren Yaffe, Rolf
Yngve, and Arthur Sze.